VOCAL DUET

AUDIO ACCESS INCLUDED
Recorded Piano Accompaniments Online

Disney
Duets for Kids

10 GREAT SONGS ARRANGED FOR VOCAL DUET

Vocal Arrangements by Joel K. Boyd

T0065938

To access companion recorded piano accompaniments online, visit:
www.halleonard.com/mylibrary

Enter Code
3437-3065-4021-2239

ISBN 978-1-4803-6901-6

Walt Disney Music Company
Wonderland Music Company, Inc.

DISTRIBUTED BY

HAL•LEONARD®
CORPORATION
7777 W. BLUEMOUND RD. P.O. BOX 13819 MILWAUKEE, WI 53213

In Australia Contact:
Hal Leonard Australia Pty. Ltd.
4 Lentara Court
Cheltenham, 3192 Victoria, Australia
Email: ausadmin@halleonard.com.au

Visit Hal Leonard Online at
www.halleonard.com

Contents

Pianist on the Recordings:
Hank Powell

The price of this publication includes access to companion recorded piano accompaniments online, for download or streaming, using the unique code found on the title page.
Visit **www.halleonard.com/mylibrary** and enter the access code.

CRUELLA DE VIL
from Walt Disney's *101 Dalmatians*

Words and Music by
Mel Leven
Vocal arrangement by
Joel K. Boyd

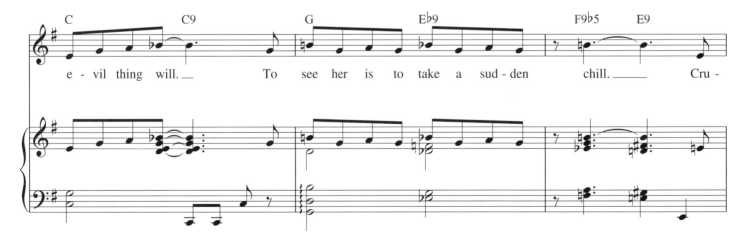

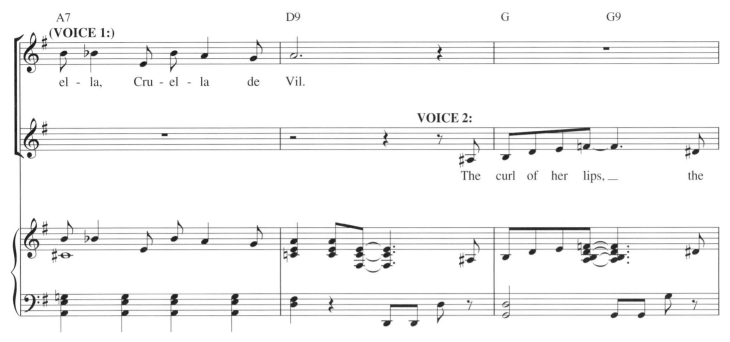

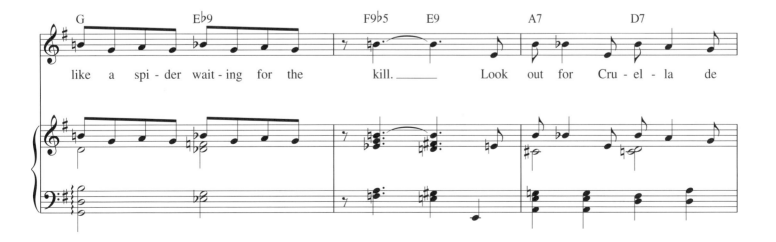

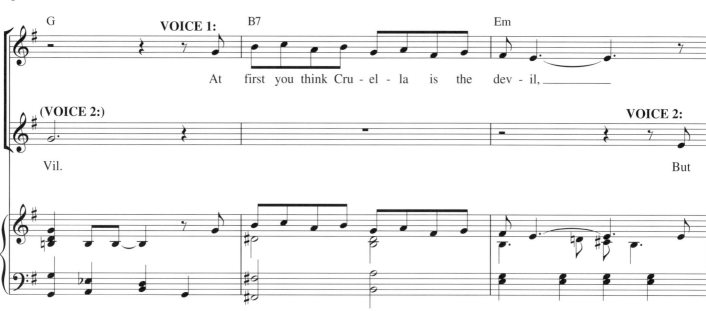

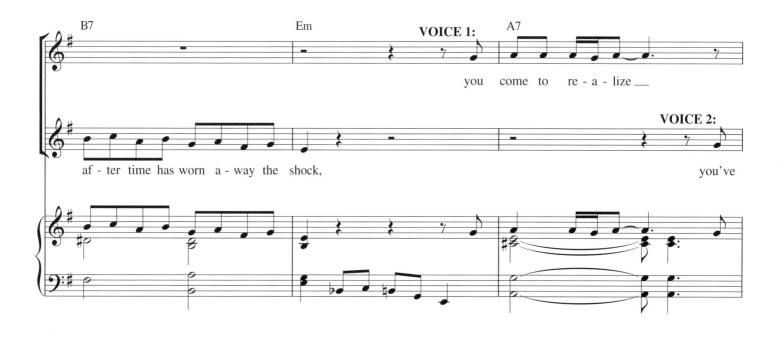

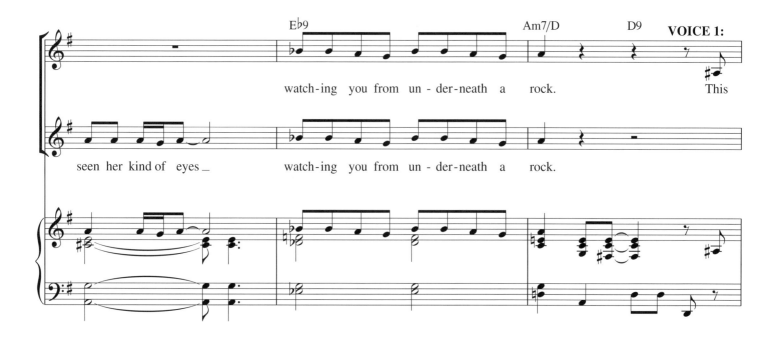

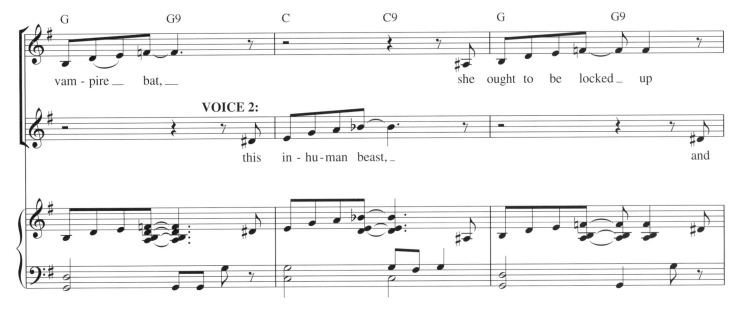

vam - pire __ bat, __ she ought to be locked __ up

VOICE 2:

this in - hu - man beast, __ and

The world was such a whole-some place un - til _____ Cru -

nev - er re - leased. _ The world was such a whole-some place un - til _____ Cru -

el - la, _____ Cru - el - la _____ de Vil. _____

el - la, _____ Cru - el - la _____ de Vil. _____

molto rit.

EV'RYBODY WANTS TO BE A CAT

from Walt Disney's *The Aristocats*

Words by Floyd Huddleston
Music by Al Rinker
Vocal arrangement by
Joel K. Boyd

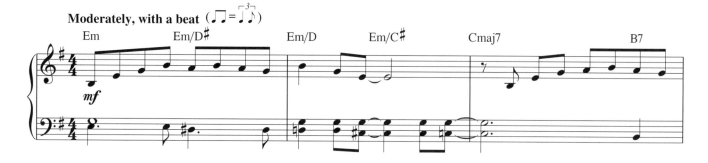

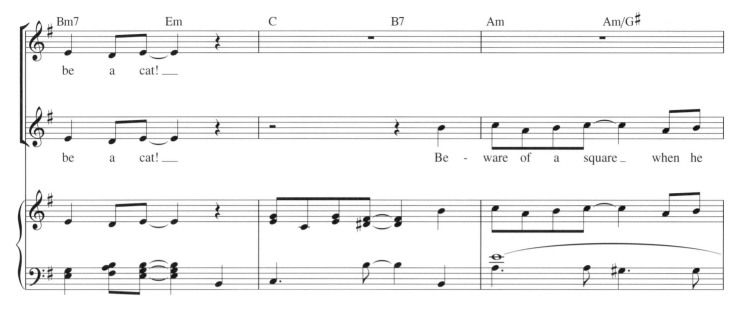

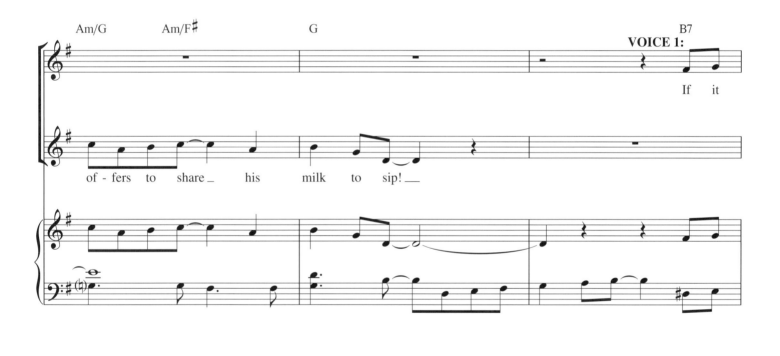

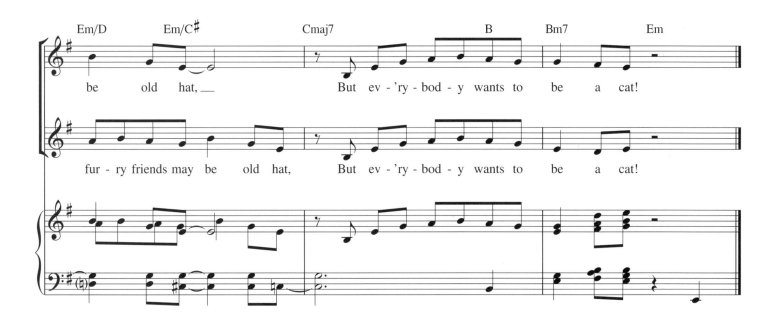

HAKUNA MATATA
from Walt Disney Pictures' *The Lion King*

Music by Elton John
Lyrics by Tim Rice
Vocal arrangement by
Joel K. Boyd

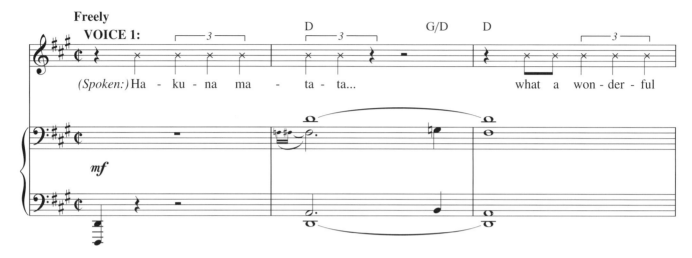

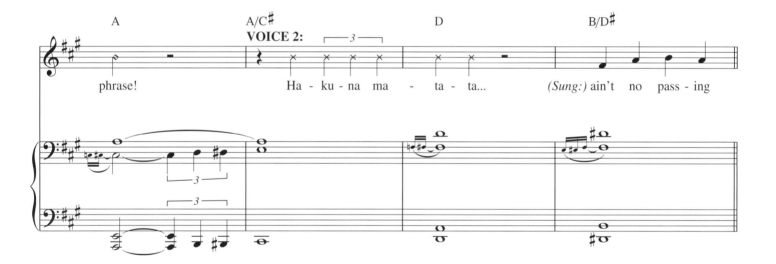

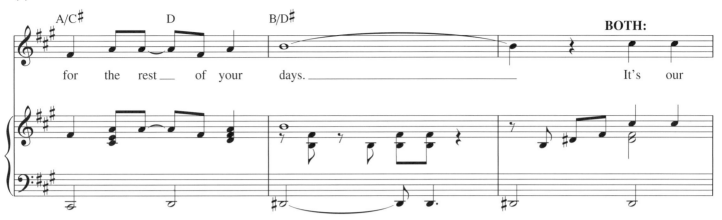

for the rest of your days. It's our

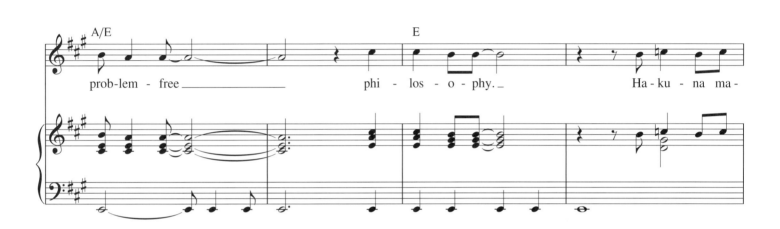

prob-lem - free phi - los - o - phy. Ha - ku - na ma-

ta - ta. Ha - ku - na ma - ta - ta...

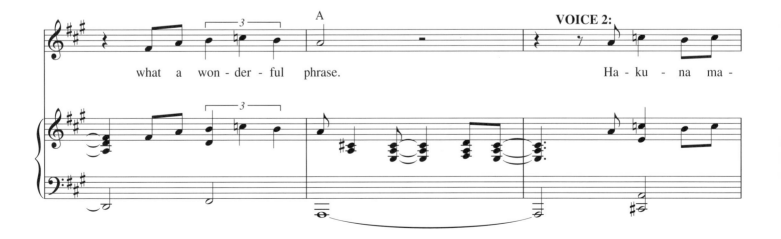

what a won - der - ful phrase. Ha - ku - na ma-

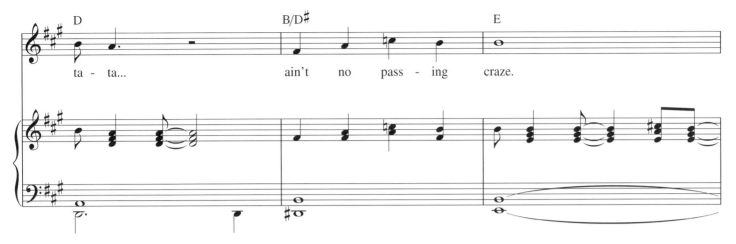

ta - ta... ain't no pass - ing craze.

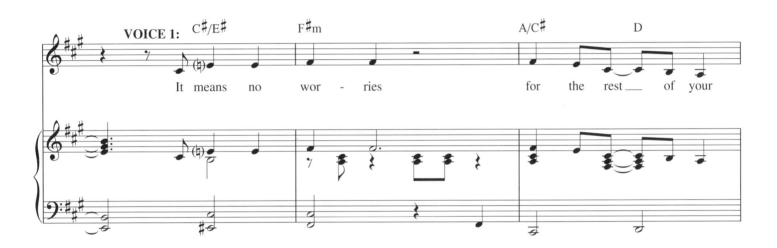

VOICE 1:

It means no wor - ries for the rest ___ of your

days. It's our prob - lem - free ___

VOICE 2:

It's our prob - lem - free ___

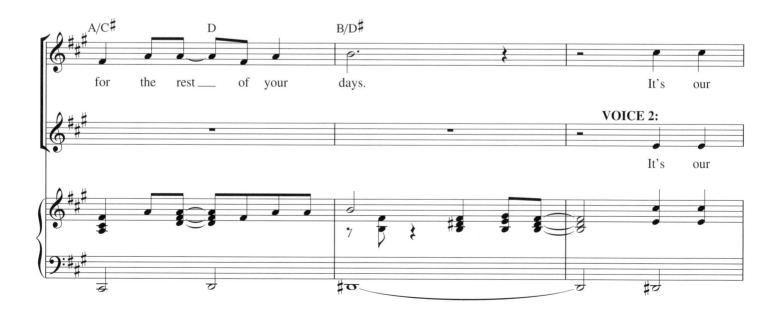

LET'S GO FLY A KITE
from Walt Disney's *Mary Poppins*

Words and Music by Richard M. Sherman
and Robert B. Sherman
Vocal arrangement by
Joel K. Boyd

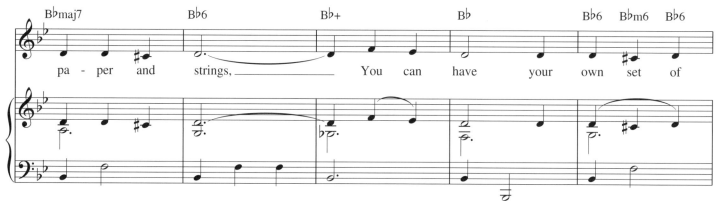

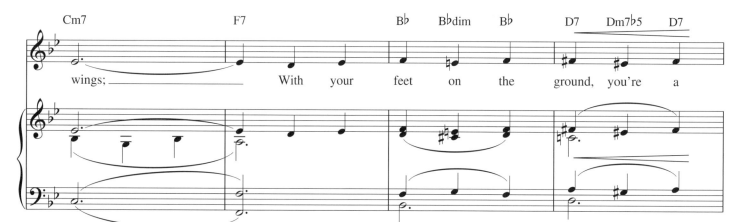

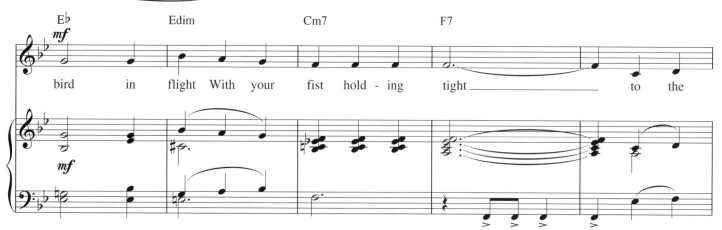

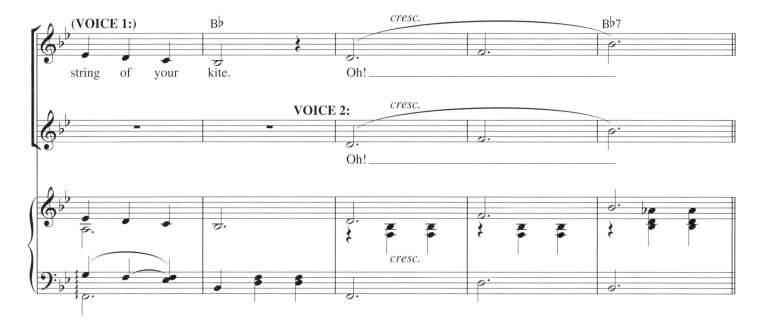

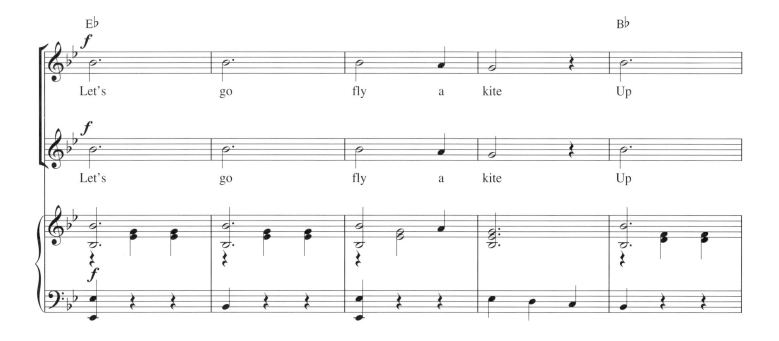

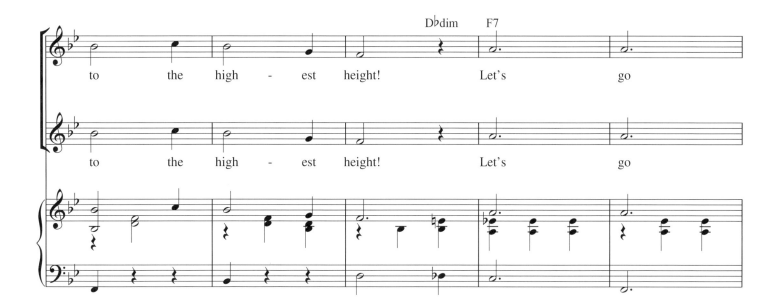

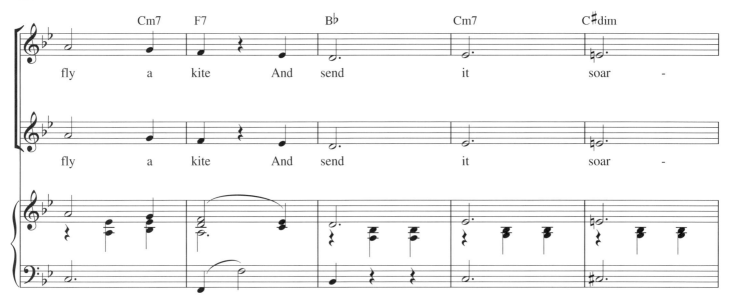

fly a kite And send it soar -

fly a kite And send it soar -

ing Up through the at - mos - phere,

ing Up through the at - mos - phere,

Up where the air is clear. Oh,

Up where the air is clear. Oh,

let's go _____ fly a kite!

let's go _____ fly a kite!

VOICE 2: *mp*

When you send it fly - ing up there, _____

mp

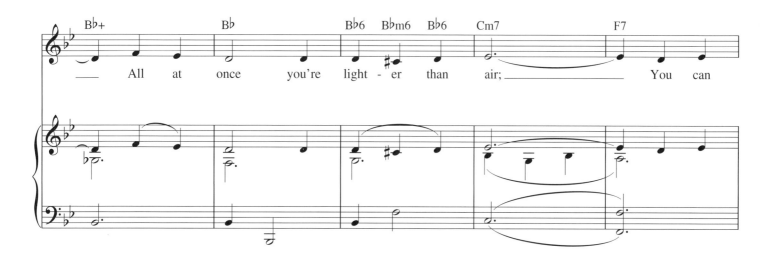

___ All at once you're light - er than air; _____ You can

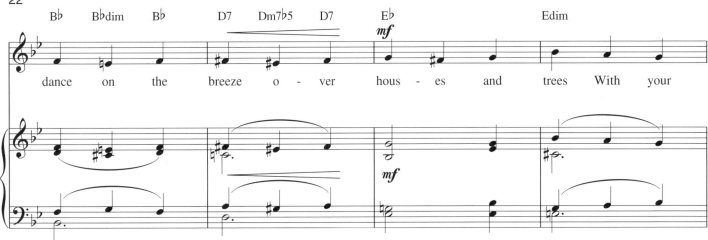

dance on the breeze o - ver hous - es and trees With your

fist hold - ing tight_____ to the string of your kite.

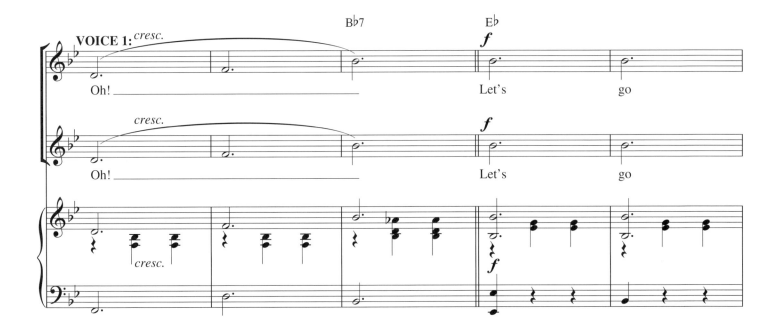

VOICE 1: *cresc.*

Oh!_____ Let's go

Oh!_____ Let's go

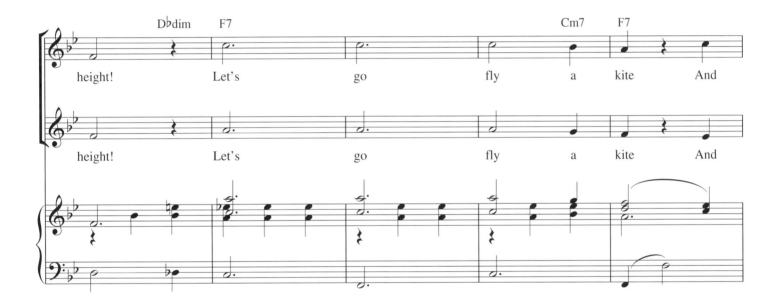

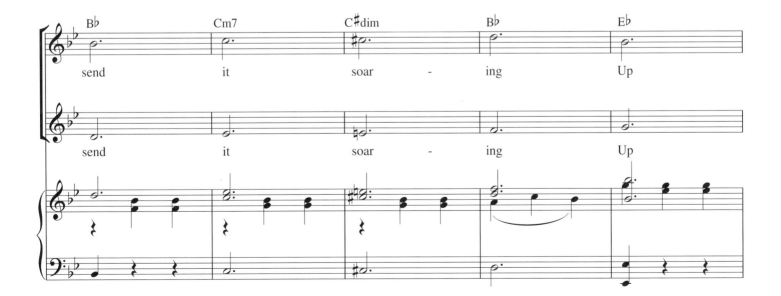

B♭
fly a kite Up to the high - est
fly a kite Up to the high - est
D♭dim F7 Cm7 F7
height! Let's go fly a kite And
height! Let's go fly a kite And
B♭ Cm7 C♯dim B♭ E♭
send it soar - ing Up
send it soar - ing Up

through the at - mos - phere, Up where the

through the at - mos - phere, Up where the

air is clear. Oh, let's go _____

air is clear. Oh, let's go _____

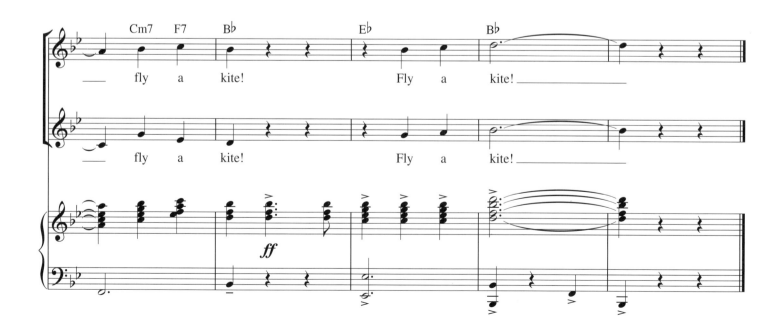

_____ fly a kite! Fly a kite! _____

fly a kite! Fly a kite! _____

THE SECOND STAR TO THE RIGHT
from Walt Disney's *Peter Pan*

Words by Sammy Cahn
Music by Sammy Fain
Vocal arrangement by
Joel K. Boyd

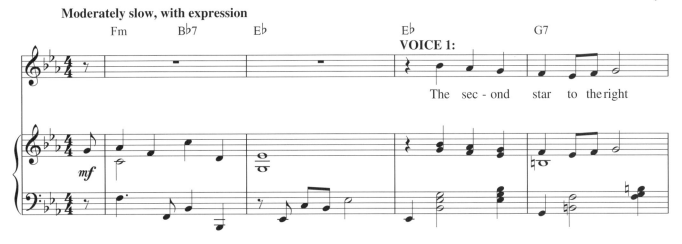

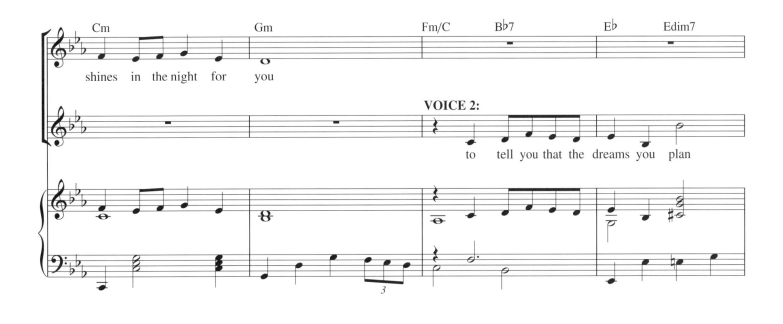

NEVER SMILE AT A CROCODILE

from Walt Disney's *Peter Pan*

Words by Jack Lawrence
Music by Frank Churchill
Vocal arrangement by
Joel K. Boyd

ag - in - ing how well you'd fit with - in his skin. Nev - er smile at a

ag - in - ing how well you'd fit with - in his skin.

croc - o - dile,

Don't be rude, nev - er mock, throw a

nev - er tip your hat and stop to talk a while. Don't be rude, nev - er mock, throw a

kill, not a rock. Clear the aisle and nev - er smile at Mis - ter Croc - o - dile.

kill, not a rock. Clear the aisle and nev - er smile at Mis - ter Croc - o - dile.

THE PERFECT NANNY
from Walt Disney's *Mary Poppins*

Words and Music by Richard M. Sherman
and Robert B. Sherman
Vocal arrangement by
Joel K. Boyd

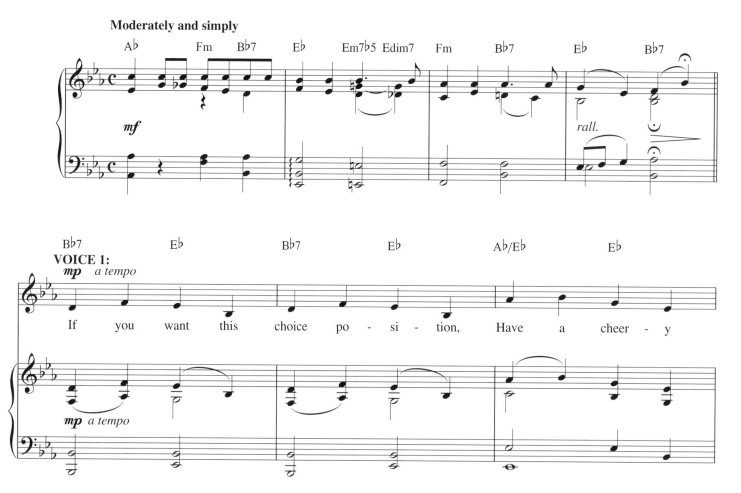

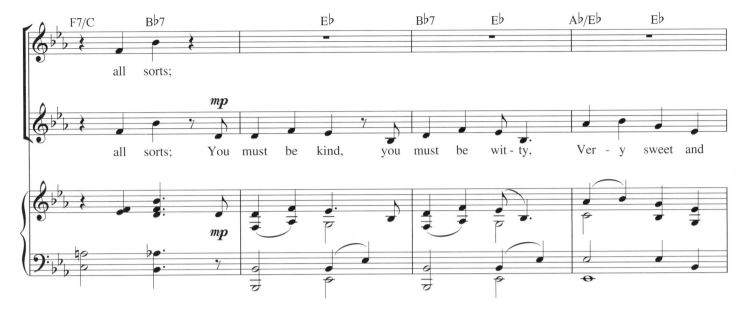

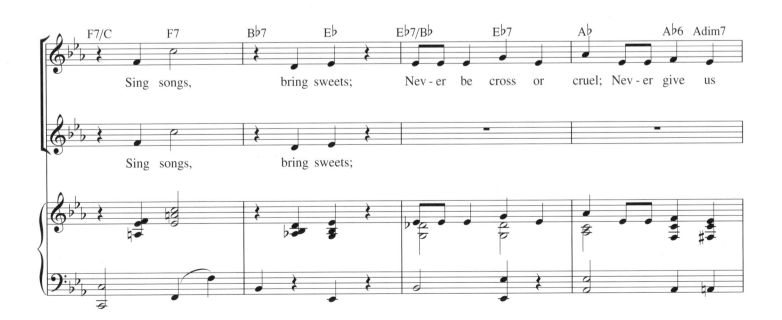

THE UNBIRTHDAY SONG
from Walt Disney's *Alice in Wonderland*

Words and Music by Mack David,
Al Hoffman and Jerry Livingston
Vocal arrangement by
Joel K. Boyd

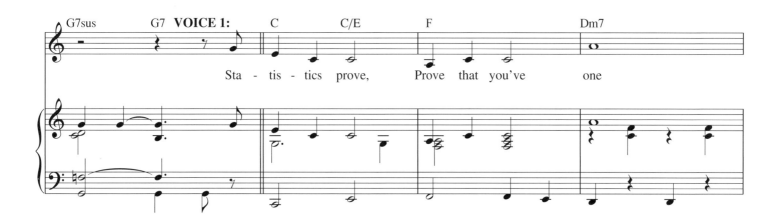

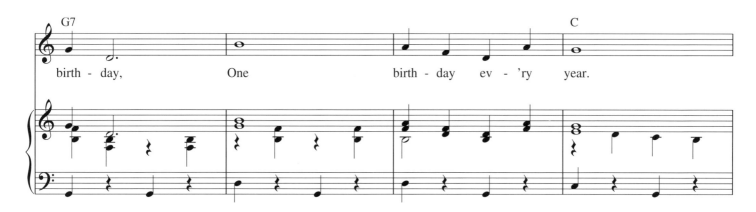

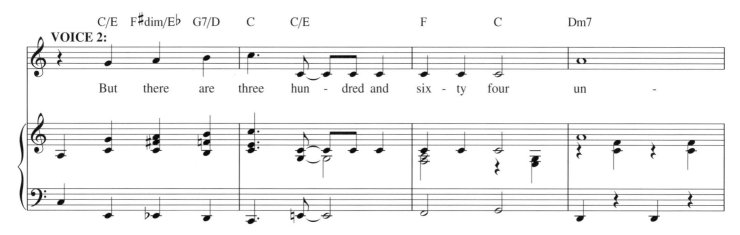

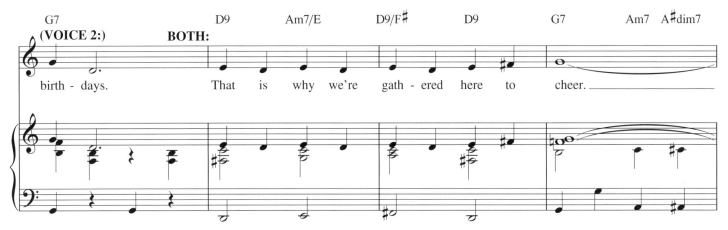

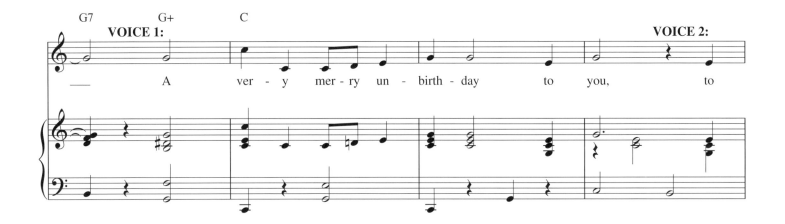

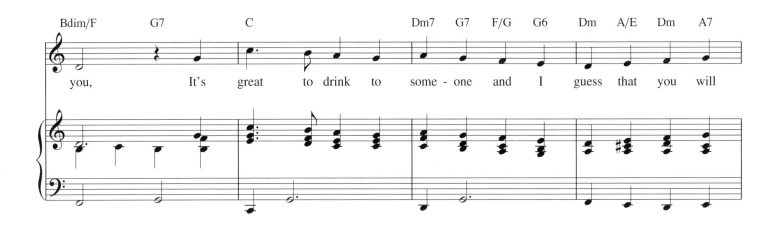

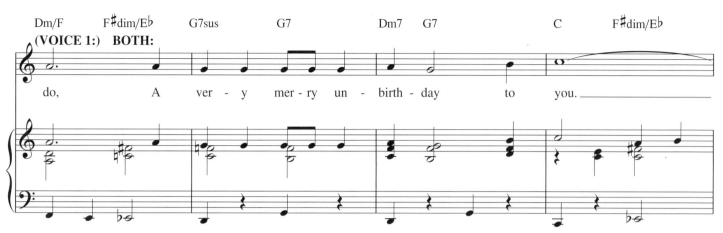

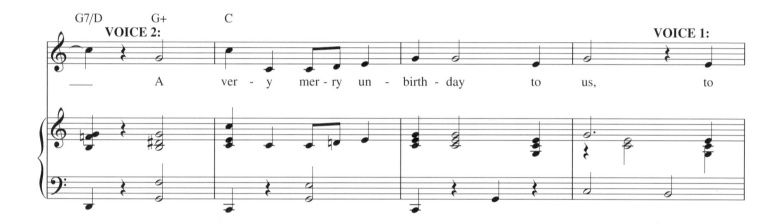

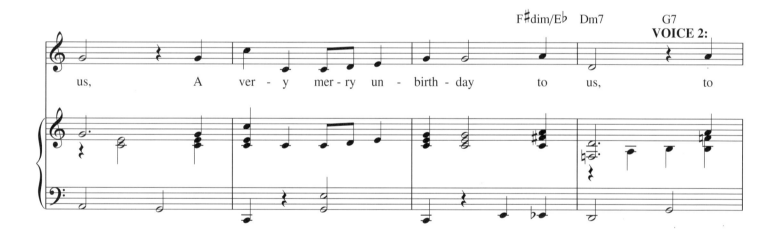

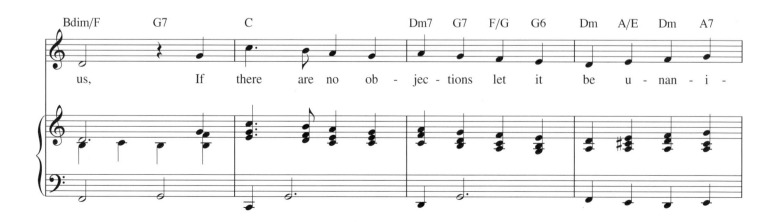

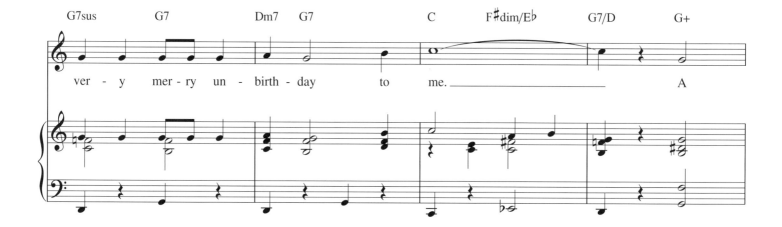

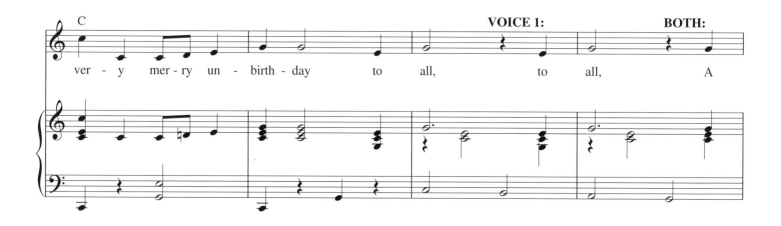

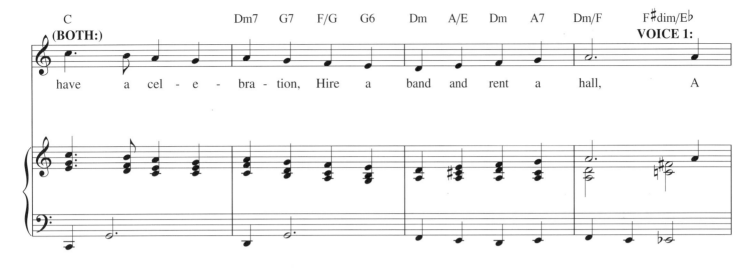

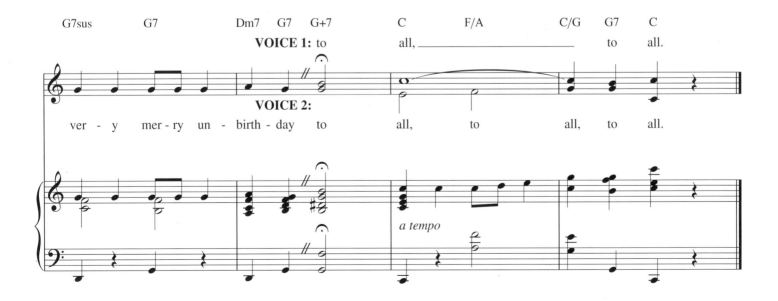

YOU'VE GOT A FRIEND IN ME

from Walt Disney's *Toy Story*

Music and Lyrics by
Randy Newman
Vocal arrangement by
Joel K. Boyd

VOICE 1:
You've got a friend in me.

VOICE 2:
You've got a friend in me.

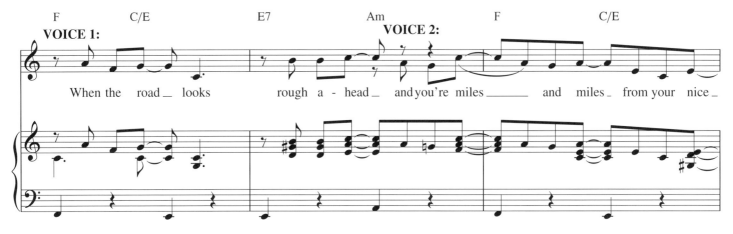

But none of them will ev - er love___ you the way___ I do,___ just

just

me and you.___ And as the years go by,___

me and you.___ our

friend - ship will nev - er die.___ You're gon - na see it's our

You're gon - na see it's our

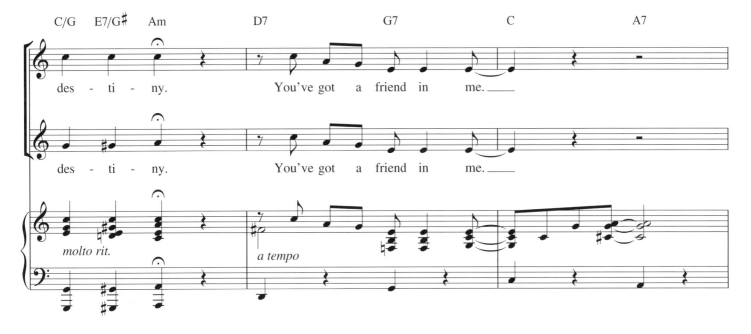

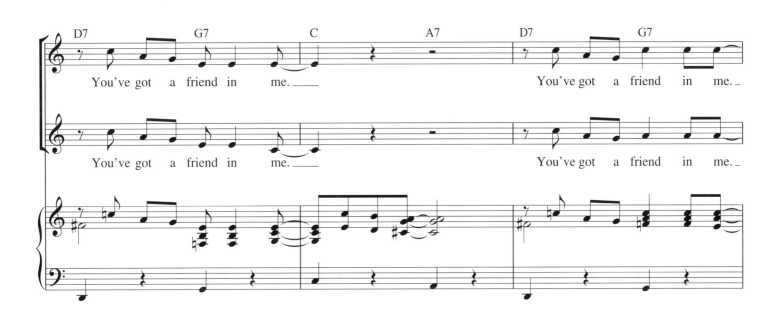

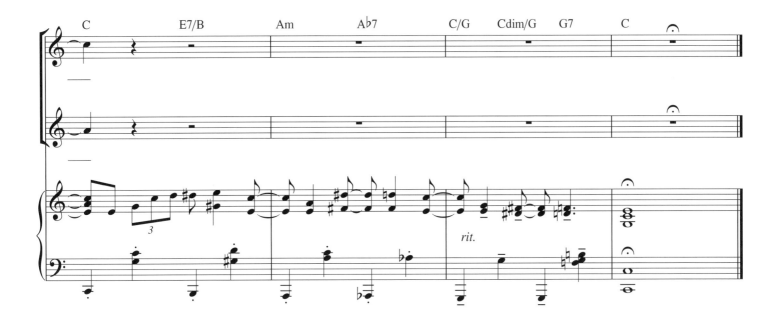

ZIP-A-DEE-DOO-DAH
from Walt Disney's *Song of the South*

Words by Ray Gilbert
Music by Allie Wrubel
Vocal arrangement by
Joel K. Boyd

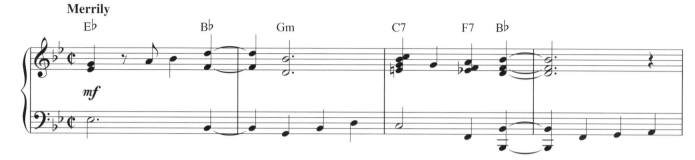

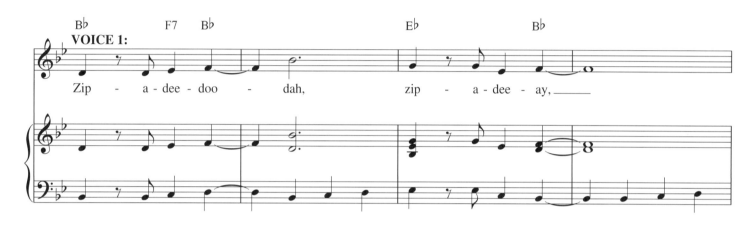

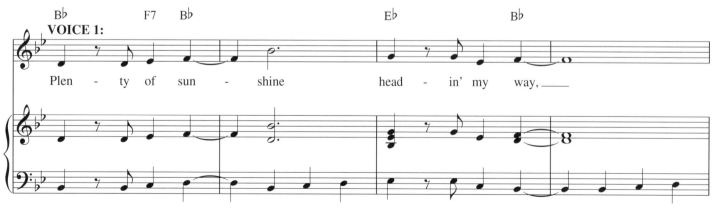

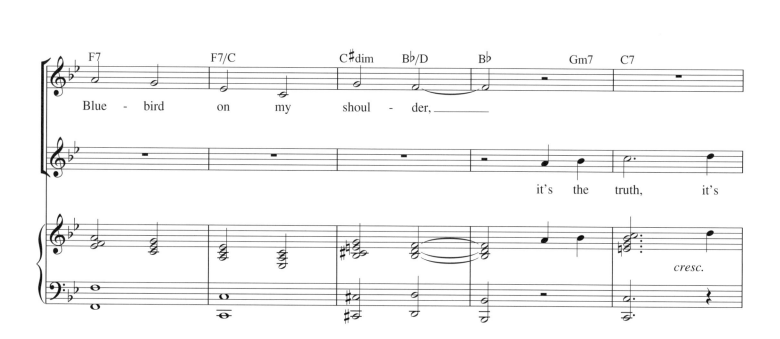

Disney Vocal Publications for Kids

DISNEY SOLOS FOR KIDS

10 classic Disney songs have been chosen as being especially appropriate solos for children. This collection of piano/vocal music comes with a companion recording, which includes full performances by a child singer, and piano accompaniment tracks for practice.

CONTENTS:

Beauty and the Beast · Chim Chim Cher-ee · A Dream Is a Wish Your Heart Makes · Ev'rybody Wants to Be a Cat · God Help the Outcasts · It's a Small World · The Lord Is Good to Me · Reflection · The Second Star to the Right · Winnie the Pooh.

00740197   Book/Audio........$19.99

MORE DISNEY SOLOS FOR KIDS

As a follow-up to the hit *Disney Solos for Kids*, here are 10 more songs that kids will love. Companion recordings include full performances and piano accompaniments for practice.

CONTENTS:

Bibbidi-Bobbidi-Boo · Can You Feel the Love Tonight · Love Is a Song · Once upon a Dream · The Perfect Nanny · When You Wish upon a Star · A Whole New World · With a Smile and a Song · You've Got a Friend in Me · Zip-A-Dee-Doo-Dah.

00740294   Book/Audio.......$19.99

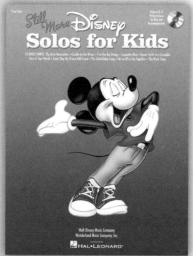

STILL MORE DISNEY SOLOS FOR KIDS

10 terrific Disney songs selected with children singers in mind! The recordings feature performances by kids who have performed in Broadway shows as well as piano accompaniments for practicing.

CONTENTS:

The Bare Necessities · Candle on the Water · I've Got No Strings · Lavender Blue (Dilly Dilly) · Never Smile at a Crocodile · Part of Your World · Some Day My Prince Will Come · The Unbirthday Song · We're All in This Together · The Work Song.

00230032   Book/Audio........$19.99

DISNEY COLLECTED KIDS' SOLOS

38 great Disney songs for kids with companion recordings of piano accompaniments for practice.

CONTENTS:

Baby Mine · The Bare Necessities · Beauty and the Beast · Bibbidi-Bobbidi-Boo · Can You Feel the Love Tonight · Candle on the Water · Chim Chim Cher-ee · Cruella De Vil · A Dream Is a Wish Your Heart Makes · Ev'rybody Wants to Be a Cat · Feed the Birds · God Help the Outcasts · I'm Late · I've Got No Strings · It's a Small World · Lavender Blue (Dilly Dilly) · Les Poissons · Let's Go Fly a Kite · The Lord Is Good to Me · Love Is a Song · Never Smile at a Crocodile · Once upon a Dream · Part of Your World · Perfect Nanny · Reflection · The Second Star to the Right · So This Is Love (The Cinderella Waltz) · Some Day My Prince Will Come · The Unbirthday Song · We're All in This Together · When I See an Elephant Fly · When You Wish upon a Star · A Whole New World · Winnie the Pooh · With a Smile and a Song · The Work Song · You've Got a Friend in Me · Zip-A-Dee-Doo-Dah.

00230066   Book/Audio........$34.99